My First Spanish Words

to See and Learn

Illustrated by David Melling
Compiled by Neil Morris

PASSPORT BOOKS
NTC/Contemporary Publishing Group

For Bosiljka, Branko and Igor Sunajko.

D.M.

Library of Congress Cataloging-in-Publication Data

My first Spanish words to see and learn / illustrated by David Melling
; compiled by Neil Morris.
     p.   cm.
    Spanish and English.
    Includes index.
    Summary: Provides vocabulary in Spanish and English, grouped by
different activities and topics and accompanied by simple
illustrations.
    ISBN 0-8442-2399-9
    1. Spanish language—Glossaries, vocabularies, etc.—Juvenile
literature.   2. English language—Glossaries, vocabularies, etc.—
Juvenile literature.   3. Picture dictionaries, Spanish—Juvenile
literature.   4. Picture dictionaries, English—Juvenile literature.
[1. Picture dictionaries, Spanish.   2. Picture dictionaries,
English.   3. Spanish language materials—Bilingual.]   I. Melling,
David, ill.   II. Morris, Neil, 1946–   .
PC4680.M9   1999
468.6'421—dc21
                                             98-37177
                                                CIP
                                                AC

Printed in Italy

This Spanish-English Edition of *My First Book of Words* originally published
in English in 1999 is published by arrangement with Oxford University Press.

This edition published 1999 by Passport Books
A division of NTC/Contemporary Publishing Group, Inc.
4255 West Touhy Avenue, Lincolnwood (Chicago), Illinois 60646-1975 U.S.A.
Text copyright © 1999 by Neil Morris
Illustrations copyright © 1999 by David Melling

International Standard Book Number: 0-8442-2399-9

16   15   14   13   12   11   10   9   8   7   6   5   4   3   2   1

Contents

Look at Me!

chest
el pecho

leg
la pierna

foot
el pie

toe
**el dedo
del pie**

elbow
el codo

back
la espalda

bottom
el trasero

finger
el dedo

tummy
el estómago

knee
la rodilla

hand
la mano

hair
el pelo

arm
el brazo

head
la cabeza

shoulders
los hombros

face
la cara

cheek
la mejilla

ear
la oreja

eye
el ojo

chin
la barbilla

mouth
la boca

teeth
los dientes

tongue
la lengua

neck
el cuello

nose
la nariz

girl
la niña

boy
el niño

5

Our House

roof
el techo

trash can
**el tanque de
la basura**

gate
la reja

stairs
la escalera

chimney
la chimenea

fence
la cerca

garage
el garaje

window
la ventana

door
la puerta

6

dog
el perro

cat
el gato

rabbit
el conejo

spider
la araña

snail
el caracol

letters
las cartas

mailbag
la bolsa de correo

leaf
la hoja

flower
la flor

tree
el árbol

Off to School

sidewalk
la acera

lamppost
el farol

playground
el patio de recreo

street
la calle

crosswalk
el cruce de peatones

school
la escuela

traffic light
el semáforo

store
la tienda

church
la iglesia

bicycle
la bicicleta

car
el coche

bus
el autobús

motorbike
la moto

fire engine
el coche de bomberos

truck
el camión

helicopter
el helicóptero

ambulance
la ambulancia

plane
el avión

Our Classroom

backpack
la mochila

lunch box
la lonchera

book
el libro

chalkboard
la pizarra

chalk
la tiza

globe
el globo terráqueo

desk
el escritorio

magnet
el imán

wastebasket
la papelera

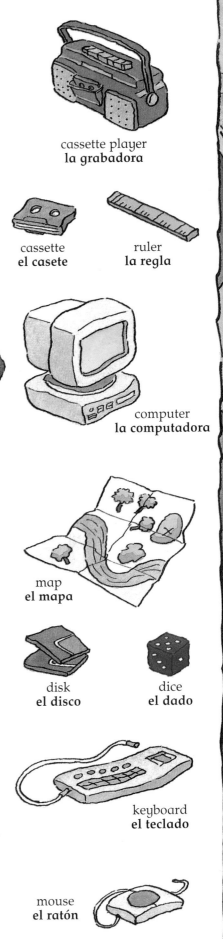

cassette player
la grabadora

cassette
el casete

ruler
la regla

computer
la computadora

map
el mapa

disk
el disco

dice
el dado

keyboard
el teclado

mouse
el ratón

11

Color Fun

black
negro

blue
azul

brown
café

green
verde

gray
gris

orange
anaranjado

pink
rosado

purple
morado

red
rojo

white
blanco

yellow
amarillo

smock
el overol

glue
la cola

painting
la pintura

paintbrush
el pincel

paints
las pinturas

pencil
el lápiz

paper
el papel

scissors
las tijeras

marker
el marcador

easel
la caballete

13

When I Grow Up

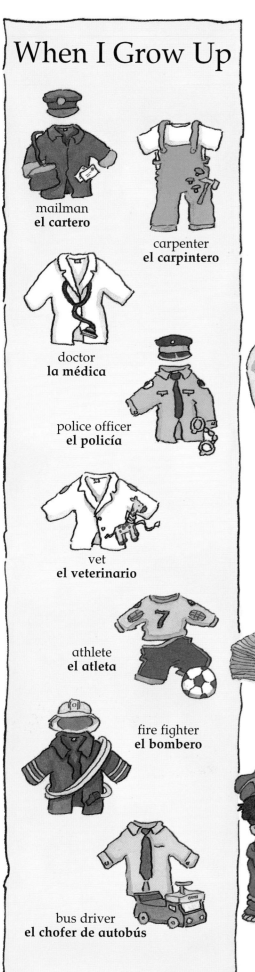

mailman
el cartero

carpenter
el carpintero

doctor
la médica

police officer
el policía

vet
el veterinario

athlete
el atleta

fire fighter
el bombero

bus driver
el chofer de autobús

engineer
el maquinista

pop star
el cantante

pilot
el piloto

dancer
la bailarina

diver
el buzo

cook
el cocinero

astronaut
el astronauta

lifeguard
el salvavidas

15

A Long Time Ago

Dinosaurs
Los dinosaurios

Tyrannosaurus Rex
el tiranosaurio Rex

Stegosaurus
el estegosaurio

Diplodocus
el diplodoco

Triceratops skeleton
el esqueleto del triceratops

fossil
el fósil

bone
el hueso

The Stone Age
La Edad de Piedra

cave
la caverna

flint
el pedernal

cave painting
la pintura de caverna

fire
el fuego

Ancient Egyptians
Los antiguos egipcios

pyramid
la pirámide

sphinx
la esfinge

Pharoah
el faraón

Ancient Romans
Los antiguos romanos

pottery
la alfarería

coins
las monedas

soldier
el soldado

Busy Shopping

shopping cart
el carrito

basket
la canasta

cash register
la caja

bread
el pan

bun
el bollo

jam
la mermelada

cereal
el cereal

potatoes
las papas

sausages
las salchichas

spaghetti
los espaguetis

milk
la leche

yogurt
el yogur

cheese
el queso

eggs
los huevos

apple
la manzana

banana
el plátano

orange
la naranja

tomato
el tomate

carrot
la zanahoria

lettuce
la lechuga

Monster Lunch

stove
la estufa

refrigerator
la nevera

washing
machine
la lavadora

saucepan
la cacerola

iron
la plancha

cup
la taza

bowl
el tazón

knife
el cuchillo

fork
el tenedor

kettle
la tetera

plate
el plato

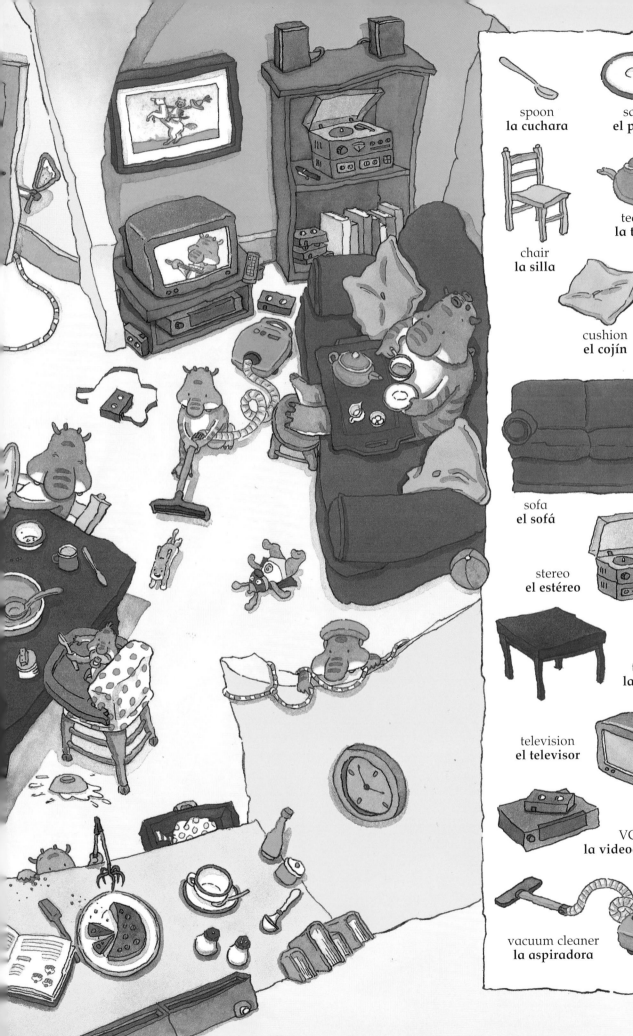

spoon
la cuchara

saucer
el platillo

chair
la silla

teapot
la tetera

cushion
el cojín

sofa
el sofá

stereo
el estéreo

table
la mesa

television
el televisor

VCR
la videocasetera

vacuum cleaner
la aspiradora

Time to Play

dollhouse
la casa de muñecas

doll
la muñeca

game
el juego

race car
el coche de carreras

robot
el robot

jigsaw puzzle
el rompecabezas

teddy bear
el osito de peluche

train set
el tren

drum
el tambor

guitar
la guitarra

keyboard
el teclado

microphone
el micrófono

trumpet
la trompeta

recorder
la flauta

cymbals
los címbalos

bells
las campanas

tambourine
la pandereta

23

On the Farm

horse
el caballo

chicken
la gallina

rooster
el gallo

duck
el pato

goose
el ganso

sheep
la oveja

goat
la cabra

pig
el cerdo

cow
la vaca

tractor
el tractor

stream
el arroyo

bridge
el puente

field
el campo

forest
el bosque

hay
la paja

hill
la colina

scarecrow
el espantapájaros

At the Beach

ball
la pelota

pail
el balde

shovel
la pala

deck chair
la silla de playa

beach umbrella
el parasol

sunscreen
la crema bronceadora

slide
el tobogán

seesaw
el subibaja

swing
el columpio

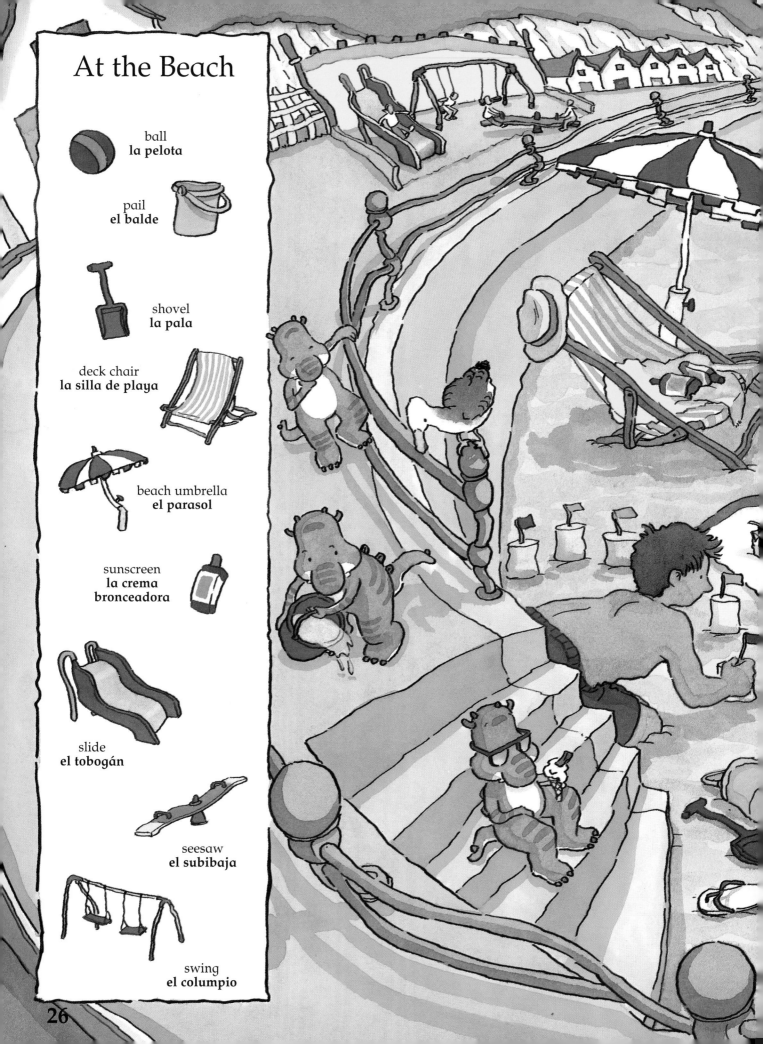

ship
el barco

lighthouse
el faro

sandcastle
**el castillo
de arena**

seagull
el gaviota

shell
la concha

crab
el cangrejo

octopus
el pulpo

starfish
la estrella de mar

seaweed
la alga marina

Birthday Party

birthday card **la tarjeta de cumpleaños**

candle **la vela**

balloon **el globo**

present **el regalo**

streamer **la cadena de papel**

noisemaker **el espantasuegras**

party hat **el gorrito de fiesta**

wand **la varita mágica**

magician **el mago**

candy
los dulces

sandwich
el bocadillo

pizza
la pizza

ice cream
el helado

chocolate
el chocolate

cookie
la galleta

straw
la paja

drink
la bebida

cake
la tarta

Animal Friends

elephant
el elefante

crocodile
el cocodrilo

giraffe
la jirafa

fish
el pez

hippopotamus
el hipopótamo

kangaroo
el canguro

monkey
el mono

koala bear
el koala

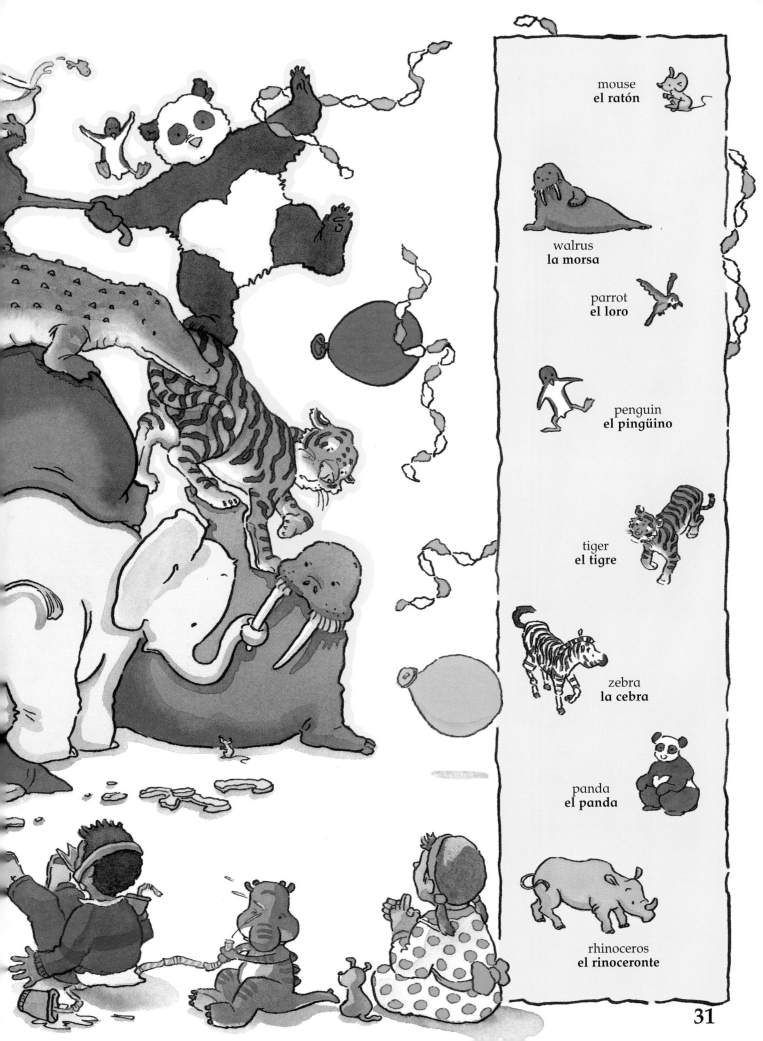

mouse
el ratón

walrus
la morsa

parrot
el loro

penguin
el pingüino

tiger
el tigre

zebra
la cebra

panda
el panda

rhinoceros
el rinoceronte

31

In the Bath

dress
el vestido

jacket
la chaqueta

sweater
el suéter

shorts
**los pantalones
cortos**

underpants
los pantaloncitos

shirt
la camisa

shoes
los zapatos

skirt
la falda

socks
los calcetines

pants
los pantalones

T-shirt
la camiseta

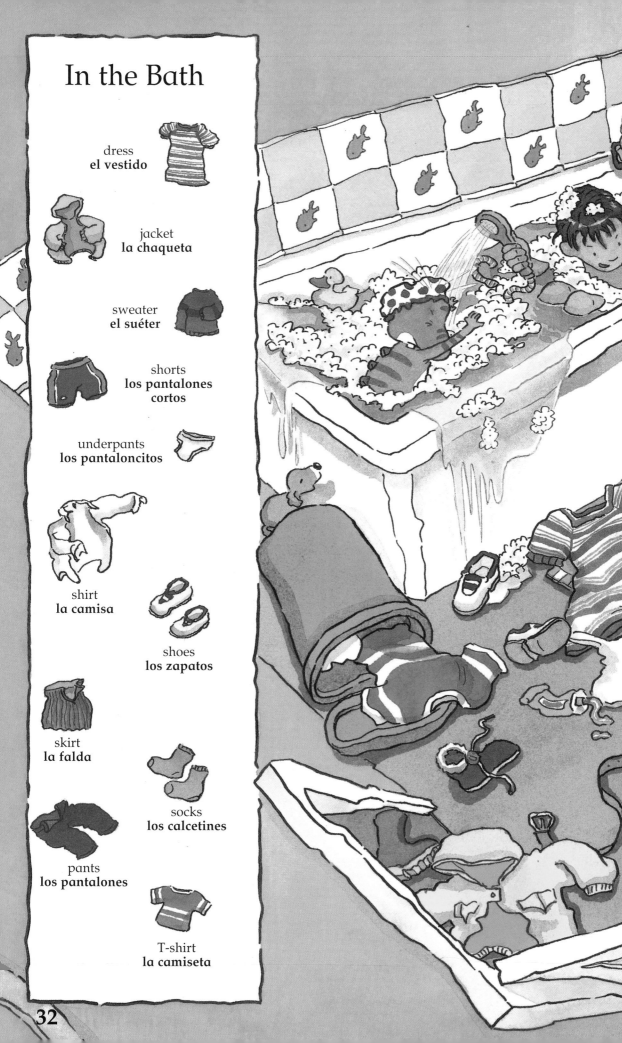

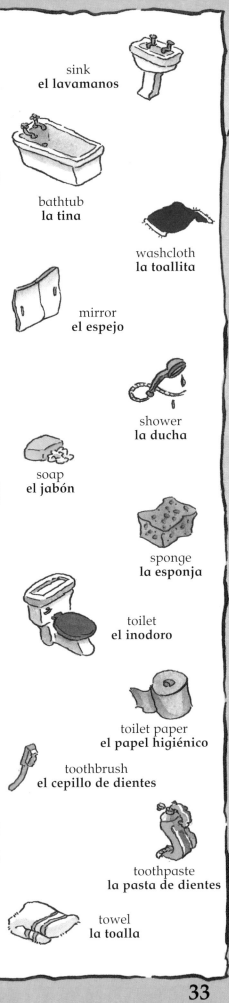

sink
el lavamanos

bathtub
la tina

washcloth
la toallita

mirror
el espejo

shower
la ducha

soap
el jabón

sponge
la esponja

toilet
el inodoro

toilet paper
el papel higiénico

toothbrush
el cepillo de dientes

toothpaste
la pasta de dientes

towel
la toalla

Time for Bed

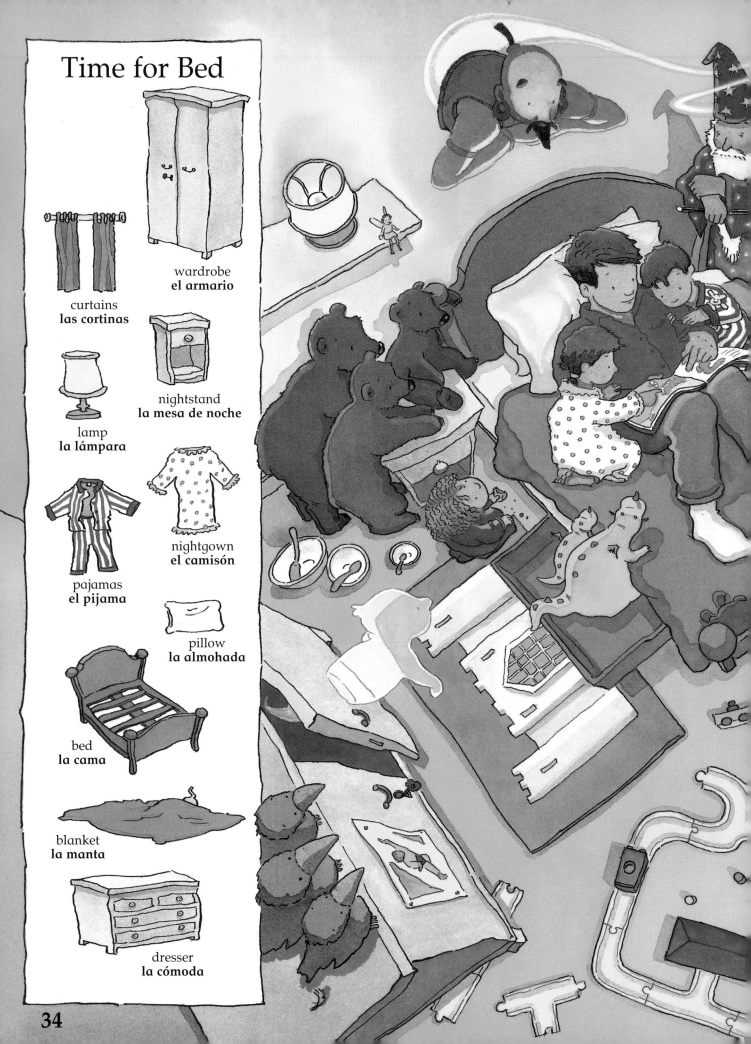

wardrobe
el armario

curtains
las cortinas

nightstand
la mesa de noche

lamp
la lámpara

nightgown
el camisón

pajamas
el pijama

pillow
la almohada

bed
la cama

blanket
la manta

dresser
la cómoda

storybook
el libro de cuentos

castle
el castillo

king
el rey

queen
la reina

genie
el genio

magic lamp
la lámpara mágica

dragon
el dragón

giant
el gigante

My ABCs

A a	ant	**la hormiga**
B b	bell	**la campana**
C c	caterpillar	**la oruga**
D d	dog	**el perro**
E e	egg	**el huevo**
F f	fish	**el pez**
G g	goat	**la cabra**
H h	helicopter	**el helicóptero**
I i	ink	**la tinta**
J j	juggler	**el malabarista**
K k	king	**el rey**
L l	ladybug	**la mariquita**
M m	mouse	**el ratón**

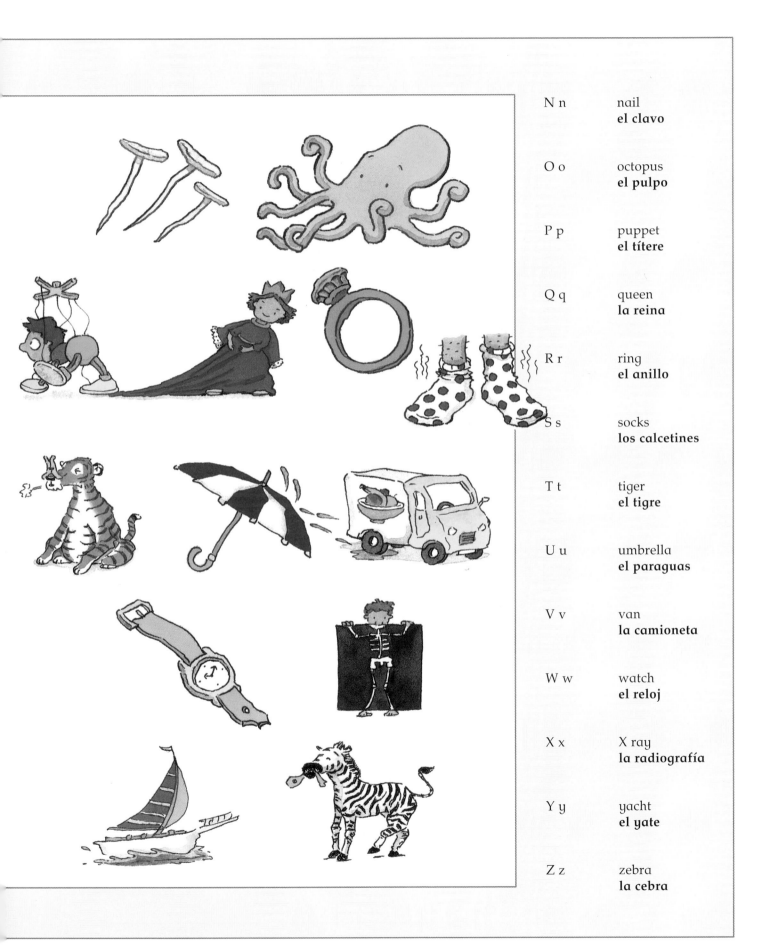

N n	nail	**el clavo**
O o	octopus	**el pulpo**
P p	puppet	**el títere**
Q q	queen	**la reina**
R r	ring	**el anillo**
S s	socks	**los calcetines**
T t	tiger	**el tigre**
U u	umbrella	**el paraguas**
V v	van	**la camioneta**
W w	watch	**el reloj**
X x	X ray	**la radiografía**
Y y	yacht	**el yate**
Z z	zebra	**la cebra**

Count 123

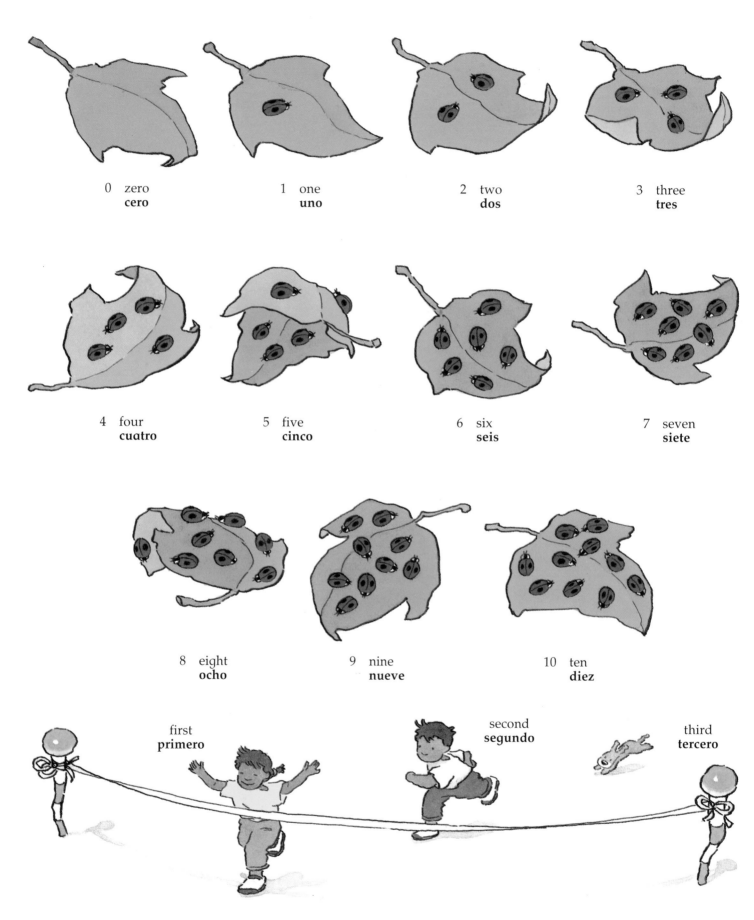

0   zero
cero

1   one
uno

2   two
dos

3   three
tres

4   four
cuatro

5   five
cinco

6   six
seis

7   seven
siete

8   eight
ocho

9   nine
nueve

10   ten
diez

first
primero

second
segundo

third
tercero

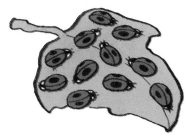

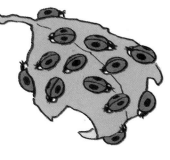

11 eleven
once

12 twelve
doce

13 thirteen
trece

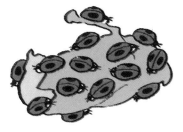

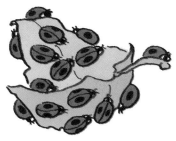

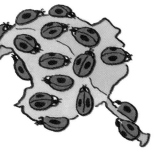

14 fourteen
catorce

15 fifteen
quince

16 sixteen
dieciséis

17 seventeen
diecisiete

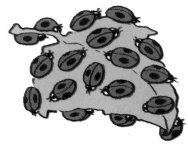

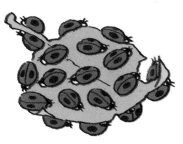

18 eighteen
dieciocho

19 nineteen
diecinueve

20 twenty
veinte

fourth
cuarto

fifth
quinto

last
último

Shapes

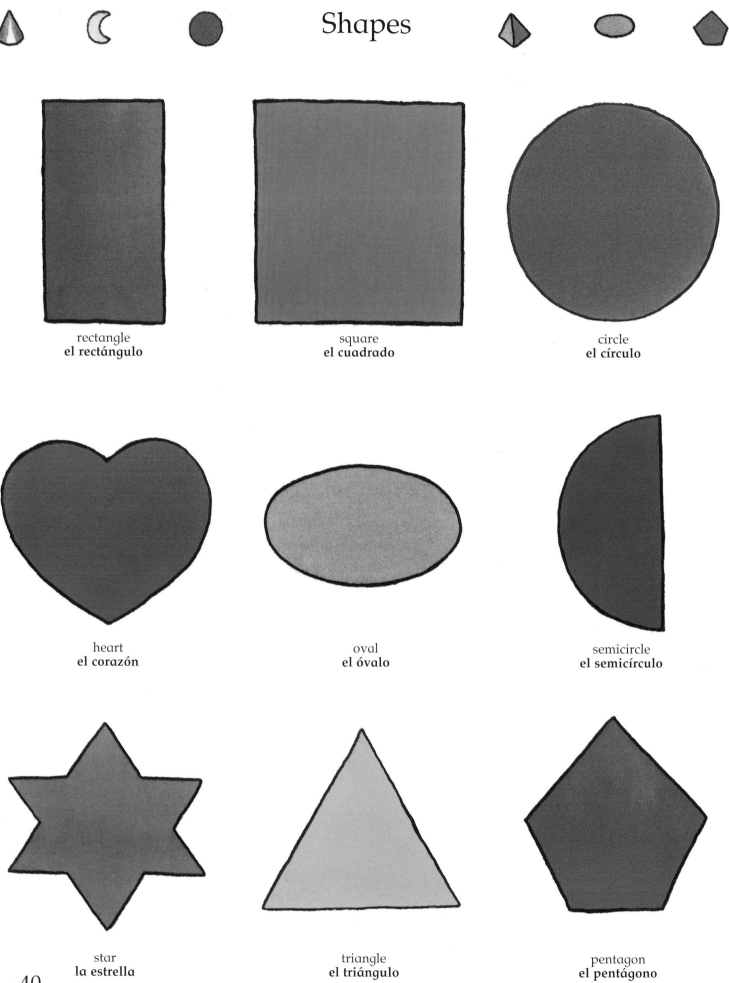

rectangle
el rectángulo

square
el cuadrado

circle
el círculo

heart
el corazón

oval
el óvalo

semicircle
el semicírculo

star
la estrella

triangle
el triángulo

pentagon
el pentágono

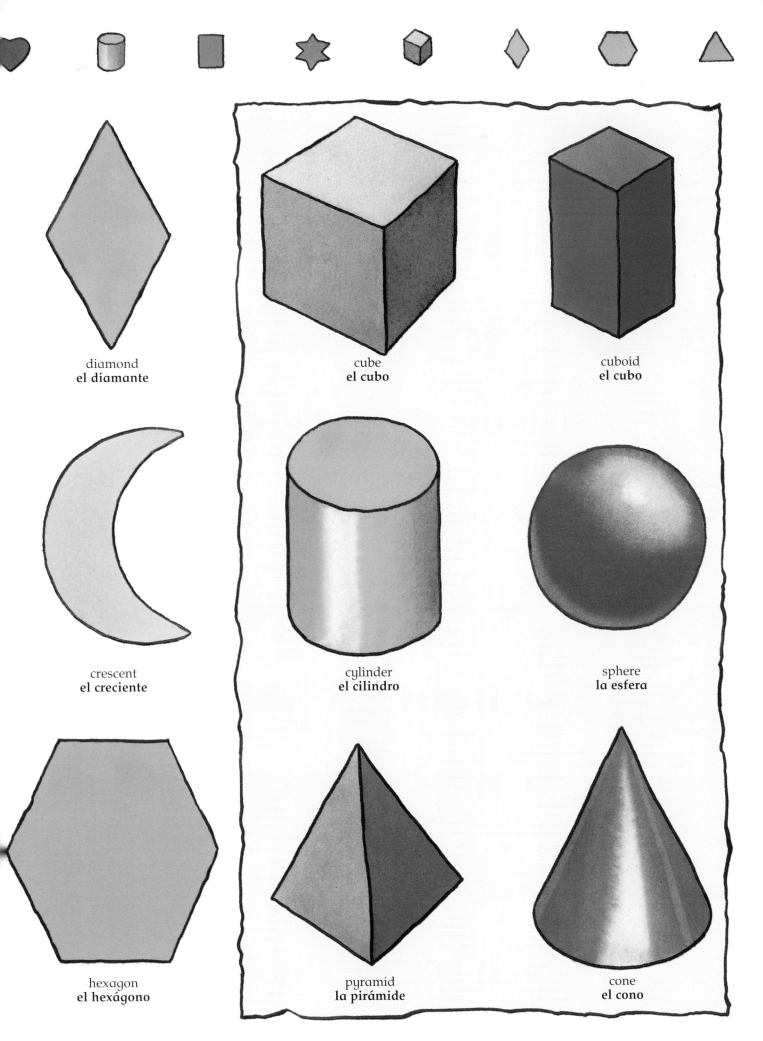

diamond
el diamante

cube
el cubo

cuboid
el cubo

crescent
el creciente

cylinder
el cilindro

sphere
la esfera

hexagon
el hexágono

pyramid
la pirámide

cone
el cono

Opposites

big/small
grande/pequeño

clean/dirty
limpio/sucio

fat/thin
gordo/delgado

full/empty
lleno/vacío

high/low
alto/bajo

hot/cold
caliente/frío

new/old
nuevo/viejo

open/closed
abierto/cerrado

dark/light
oscuro/claro

fast/slow
rápido/lento

happy/sad
feliz/triste

heavy/light
pesado/ligero

long/short
largo/corto

more/less
más/menos

same/different
igual/diferente

wet/dry
mojado/seco

43

Weather

It's cloudy.
Está nublado.

It's sunny.
Hace sol.

It's raining.
Está lloviendo.

It's snowing.
Está nevando.

It's windy.
Hace viento.

It's foggy.
Está brumoso.

44

It's 8 AM.
Son las ocho de la mañana.

It's 10 AM.
Son las diez de la mañana.

It's noon.
Es mediodía.

It's 2 PM.
Son las dos de la tarde.

It's 4 PM.
Son las cuatro de la tarde.

It's 6 PM.
Son las seis de la tarde.

English-Spanish Index

five	cinco	38
flint	el pedernal	17
flower	la flor	7
foggy	brumoso	44
foot	el pie	4
forest	el bosque	25
fork	el tenedor	20
fossil	el fósil	16
four	cuatro	38
fourteen	catorce	39
fourth	cuarto	39
full	lleno	42
game	el juego	22
garage	el garaje	6
gate	la reja	6
genie	el genio	35
giant	el gigante	35
giraffe	la jirafa	30
girl	la niña	5
globe	el globo terráqueo	10
glue	la cola	13
goat	la cabra	24, 36
goose	el ganso	24
gray	gris	12
green	verde	12
guitar	la guitarra	23
hair	el pelo	4
hand	la mano	4
happy	feliz	43
hay	la paja	25
head	la cabeza	4
heart	el corazón	40
heavy	pesado	43
helicopter	el helicóptero	9, 36
hexagon	el hexágono	41
high	alto	42
hill	la colina	25
hippopotamus	el hipopótamo	30
horse	el caballo	24
hot	caliente	42
house	la casa	6–7
ice cream	el helado	29
ink	la tinta	36
iron	la plancha	20
jacket	la chaqueta	32
jam	la mermelada	18
jigsaw puzzle	el rompecabezas	22
juggler	el malabarista	36
kangaroo	el canguro	30
kettle	la tetera	20
keyboard (music)	el teclado	23
keyboard (PC)	el teclado	11
king	el rey	35, 36
knee	la rodilla	4
knife	el cuchillo	20
koala bear	el koala	30
ladybug	la mariquita	36
lamp	la lámpara	34
lamppost	el farol	8
last	último	39
leaf	la hoja	7
leg	la pierna	4
less	menos	43
letters	las cartas	7
lettuce	la lechuga	19
lifeguard	el salvavidas	15
light (bright)	claro	43
light (weight)	ligero	43
lighthouse	el faro	27
long	largo	43
low	bajo	42

lunch	el almuerzo	20–21
lunch box	la lonchera	10
magic lamp	la lámpara mágica	35
magician	el mago	28
magnet	el imán	10
mailbag	la bolsa de correo	7
mailman	el cartero	14
map	el mapa	11
marker	el marcador	13
microphone	el micrófono	23
milk	la leche	19
mirror	el espejo	33
monkey	el mono	30
more	más	43
motorbike	la moto	9
mouse (animal)	el ratón	31, 36
mouse (PC)	el ratón	11
mouth	la boca	5
nail	el clavo	37
neck	el cuello	5
new	nuevo	42
nightgown	el camisón	34
nightstand	la mesa de noche	34
nine	nueve	38
nineteen	diecinueve	39
noisemaker	el espantasuegras	28
nose	la nariz	5
numbers	los números	38–39
octopus	el pulpo	27, 37
old	viejo	42
one	uno	38
open	abierto	42
opposites	los opuestos	42–43
orange (color)	anaranjado	12
orange (fruit)	la naranja	19
oval	el óvalo	40
pail	el balde	26
paintbrush	el pincel	13
painting	la pintura	13
paints	las pinturas	13
pajamas	el pijama	34
panda	el panda	31
pants	los pantalones	32
paper	el papel	13
parrot	el loro	31
party hat	el gorrito de fiesta	28
pencil	el lápiz	13
penguin	el pingüino	31
pentagon	el pentágono	40
Pharoah	el faraón	17
pig	el cerdo	24
pillow	la almohada	34
pilot	el piloto	15
pink	rosado	12
pizza	la pizza	29
plane	el avión	9
plate	el plato	20
playground	el patio de recreo	8
police officer	el policía	14
pop star	el cantante	15
potatoes	las papas	18
pottery	la alfarería	17
present	el regalo	28
puppet	el títere	37
purple	morado	12
pyramid (Egypt)	la pirámide	17
pyramid (shape)	la pirámide	41
queen	la reina	35, 37
rabbit	el conejo	7
race car	el coche de carreras	22
raining	lloviendo	44

47